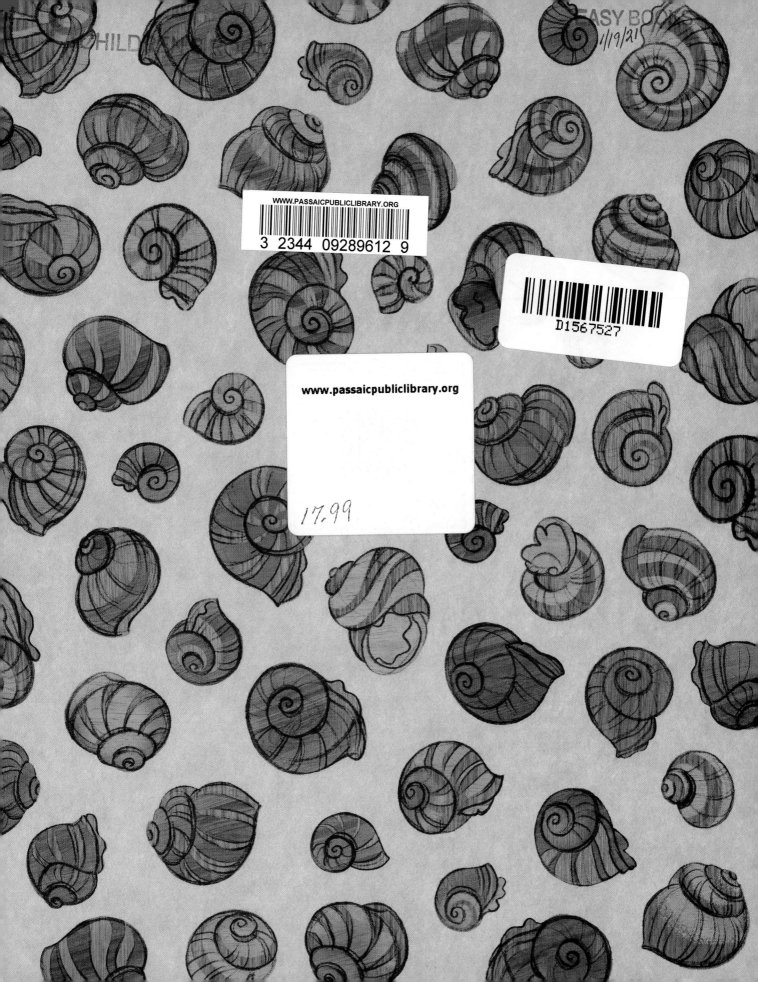

Let's Eat Snails!

Barbara Barcellona Smith

Illustrations by Karen Lewis

To the original culinary adventurers,
my parents Giuseppe and Emily Barcellona.
Love, Barbara

NewSouth Books
105 S. Court Street
Montgomery, AL 36104

Publisher Cataloging-in-Publication Data
Names: Smith, Barbara Barcellona, author. | Lewis, Karen, illustrator.
Title: Let's eat snails! / by Barbara Barcellona Smith; illus. by Karen Lewis.
Description: Montgomery : NewSouth Books, [2021] |
Audience: Grades 4–6 | Audience: Ages 7–12.
Identifiers: LCCN 2020946228 | ISBN 9781588384034 (hardback)
Subjects: Food–Culture–Juvenile literature.
| Cooking food–Juvenile nonfiction. |
Customs, traditions, anthropology–Social
science–Juvenile literature. | Cooking
for kids–Cooking.

Printed in the United States of
America by Jostens

Andiamo!

yelled Mr. Barcellona.

"What's your dad saying? And why is he shouting at us?" asked Margie. Laughing, I responded, "My dad's from Italy, so he's speaking Italian. He just said, 'Let's go.'

As for the shouting ~ that's how we talk. You'll get used to it ~ my whole family shouts!"

While running to catch up with my dad, Margie asked, "Are we really going on a snail hunt?"

"Yep!" I replied.

"Are we really picking them to make snail stew?" she asked.

"Yep!" I replied.

Our one-acre backyard was snail paradise.

Beyond the decorated patio and manicured lawn was our large garden.

Growing in it you would find giant zucchini, green *and* purple string beans, and, of course, snails ~ lots and lots of snails!

"Have *you* ever eaten a snail?" Margie asked me, as if afraid of the answer.

"Yep!" I replied as I began filling up my five-gallon bucket with slippery snails.

"You are GROSS!" Margie shrieked, then covered her mouth in disgust.

I waved one of the outstretched snails in Margie's face. "I know! Isn't it awesome?" I laughed.

"Stop it!" my dad shouted at me. "Stop teasing your friend. You invited her over to show her how to pick, purify, prepare, and eat snails ~ not scare her!"

Well, not exactly, I thought to myself.

That's what I told my dad so he would let her spend the night. In fact, most friends had to agree to help me finish some unpleasant chore, since I had so many, if they ever wanted to come over and spend the night.

But I was always polite enough to forewarn them about the *real* potential for unsavory sights such as the dead still-feathered game birds and rabbits or smelly fish in the Barcellona kitchen sink should they bravely say, "Yes."

"Mr. Barcellona, I thought I would be able to do this, but I don't think I want to touch or eat a snail," said Margie.

I thought Margie was starting to look a bit green when my dad said, "Nonsense!

When you go back to school on Monday you can tell all your friends you are on your way to becoming a top European-trained chef!

Many different kinds of people from all over the world eat snails. The French call them *escargot* and they are quite expensive to purchase at fine restaurants."

"I've heard of *escargot*," Margie said.

"*Bene!*" Dad replied.

Make sure you only pick snails from a safe place, like my yard, where there is no chance that anyone has used snail poison ...

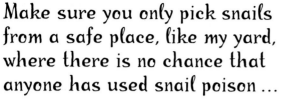

and never, ever eat a RAW snail.

Always search for the larger, mature snails, and simply place them in a big five-gallon bucket, like this.

He lifted the screen mesh cover and added the snails to the well-populated bucket.

"When Nina and I collect a few pounds of snails, I often have friends over for a delicious snail stew ~ as we are doing tonight," he said.

I showed Dad my bucket and he agreed that, between the three of us, we had enough snails to move on to the next step: purifying them.

Nina, you have done this before. Show Margie what we do next.

I merged our three buckets of snails into one larger bucket that already had small holes drilled into it and then placed it in the remote corner of the patio my dad called the Barcellona Snail Farm.

We sprayed the snails down with a fine mist of water for about a minute, aiming the nozzle at the screens.

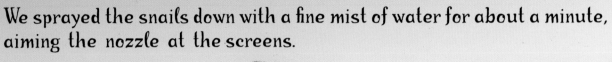

I grabbed a different bucket from the corner.

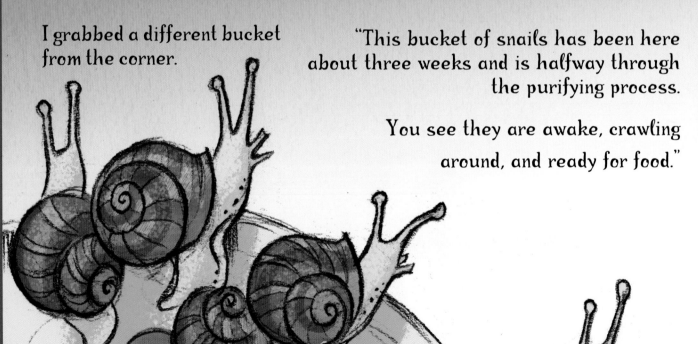

"This bucket of snails has been here about three weeks and is halfway through the purifying process.

You see they are awake, crawling around, and ready for food."

I smiled and reassured her, "You don't have to watch us cook them if you don't want to."

Pulling herself together, Margie replied, "My family has never done anything like this before. I can't believe I am admitting this, but even though I still think it's gross, this has actually been really interesting."

Margie noticed the smile on my face and asked,

I opened the patio door and we walked into our spacious, Mediterranean-tiled kitchen.

Margie marveled at a giant tree growing up through the glass-walled atrium in the center of our house. Its branches reached for open sky through the rooftop!

My mother, smiling, greeted us and said,

Hello, girls! I'm ready to show you how to prepare the snail stew.

A savory-smelling pot of seasoned carrots, celery, potatoes, and bell peppers gently bubbled in a tomato sauce on the stovetop.

Next to it, a giant, deep pan full of garlic and onions sautéed in olive oil sweetened the air.

And next to that, a roaring pot of boiling water sent droplets crackling into the fire.

We were ready to cook the snails.

Dad lightly misted the ready-to-cook snails before bringing them to the kitchen, so they were out of their shells and crawling around.

It's best to drop them into the boiling water when they are crawling because they will be easier to hook out of the shells when it's time to eat.

Dad dropped the snails into the giant pot of boiling water and let them cook for twenty minutes.

Looking into the murky water, Margie couldn't help but question,

Forgive me for asking, Mr. Barcellona, but how in the world did you ever learn to eat snails?

Chuckling at Margie, who was still staring at the green pot of bugs, my dad replied,

"I grew up number three out of six children in a poor family on the small Italian island of Sicily.

I didn't go to school much because I spent most of my time helping my family to make a living. We raised sheep and hunted small game for dinner, like rabbits and doves. And, of course, we sometimes gathered snails just as we did today."

"Wow, my dad grew up in Orange County eating meatloaf and hot dogs," Margie said in amazement.

"I certainly never ate hot dogs until I moved to America, and I've never quite liked meatloaf," my father said. "But I did try it! And I hope you will be as open-minded about our Italian-style snail stew."

"Don't worry, Margie," my mom said. "We first have to clean this yucky-looking pot before we can add the snails to the stew."

As the dinner guests arrived and took their places at our large dining room table, I introduced my blond-haired friend. Many guests asked Margie if she liked snails.

I'm going to find out tonight!

Margie said bravely.

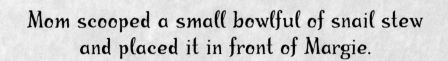

Mom scooped a small bowlful of snail stew
and placed it in front of Margie.

My dad handed her a small hooked skewer
and quickly showed her how to use it
should she come across a snail still
curled up in its shell.

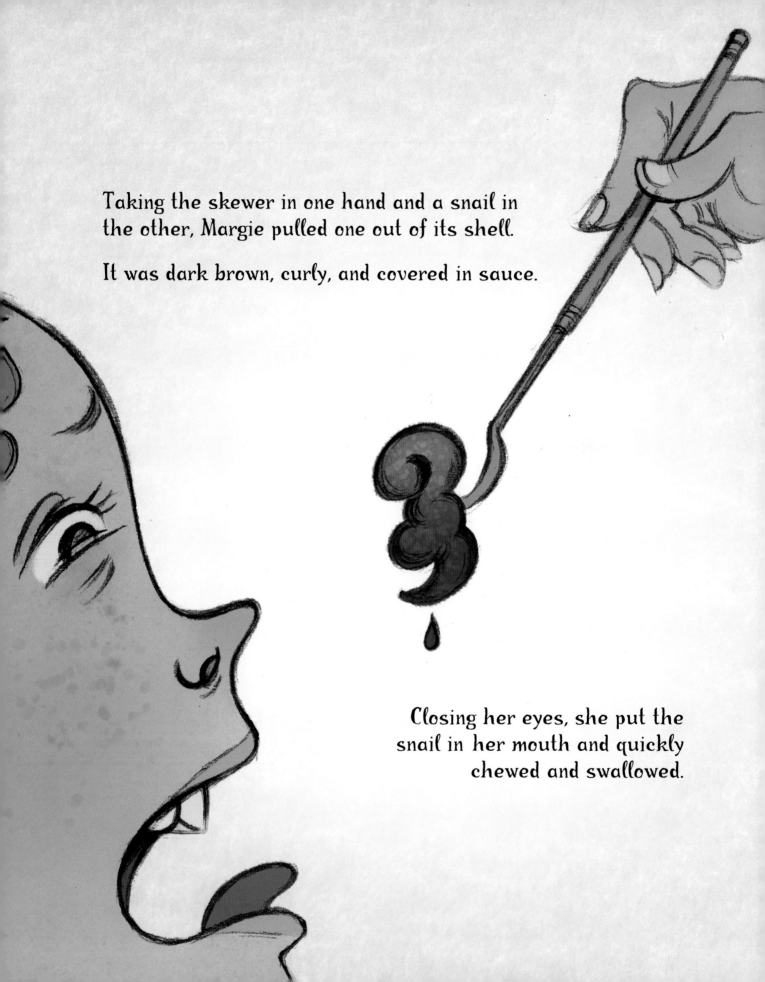

Taking the skewer in one hand and a snail in the other, Margie pulled one out of its shell.

It was dark brown, curly, and covered in sauce.

Closing her eyes, she put the snail in her mouth and quickly chewed and swallowed.

All eyes were on her, waiting for her reaction.

Margie scrunched her mouth up toward her nose and said,

"*Well . . . it was squishy.*"

She looked into the bowl of snails and continued.

"*Well . . . it was saucy.*"

Disclaimer: Kids, we need to remember to NEVER eat raw or partially cooked snails—this could make you very sick! Always have an adult help you make sure that the foods you eat, like snails, have been cooked properly.

Parents, the consumption of raw or undercooked eggs, meat, poultry, seafood, or shellfish, including snails, may increase your risk of food-borne illness. Please take a moment to discuss with the children who have read or listened to my story the health risks associated with the consumption of raw or undercooked foods. Remind children to always have adult supervision when preparing or eating foods that must be cooked to certain temperatures.

About the Author and This Story:

Barbara Barcellona Smith grew up on the central coast of California with her Italian father, Giuseppe Barcellona, and Puerto Rican-Cuban-Lebanese mother, Emily. It was nothing to come home from school to find dead doves, rabbits, or whatever her hunter-dad shot that day. All friends knew NOT to say "Gross!" no matter what they saw in the kitchen sink unless they wanted a twenty-minute lecture from the Sicilian Godfather on manners and expanding one's horizons!

Barbara's ethnic household was quite unique, providing her with a lifetime supply of strange, entertaining, and valuable stories like *Let's Eat Snails!* to share with young readers. In

Judy McCall

addition to writing, Barbara has worked as a radio promotions director, an award-winning television commercial production coordinator, and a corporate marketer. She has a degree in journalism/public relations from California Polytechnic State University, SLO. She was an English as a Second Language educator and now lives in Enterprise, Alabama.

Let's Eat Snails! is her first book. It takes her young readers on a culinary journey where they might never have had the opportunity to venture. In addition to whetting children's appetites for new and unfamiliar dishes, *Let's Eat Snails!* is also a cultural window allowing children to peer into the lives of ethnic neighbors who are a large portion of American society. This book is a metaphor for all sorts of cultural things we're afraid to try, then try and find we enjoy!

About the Illustrator:

Karen Lewis grew up in the rainy northwest, where there are lots and lots of banana slugs. Though she greatly admires Mr. Barcellona's garden, she has not been tempted to make slug stew, or banana slug bread for that matter. She has a garden of her own in Seattle, where she resides with her husband, young son, two cats, eight chickens, and thousands of honey bees. They live smack in the middle of the city and pretend to have a farm. The neighbors believe them!

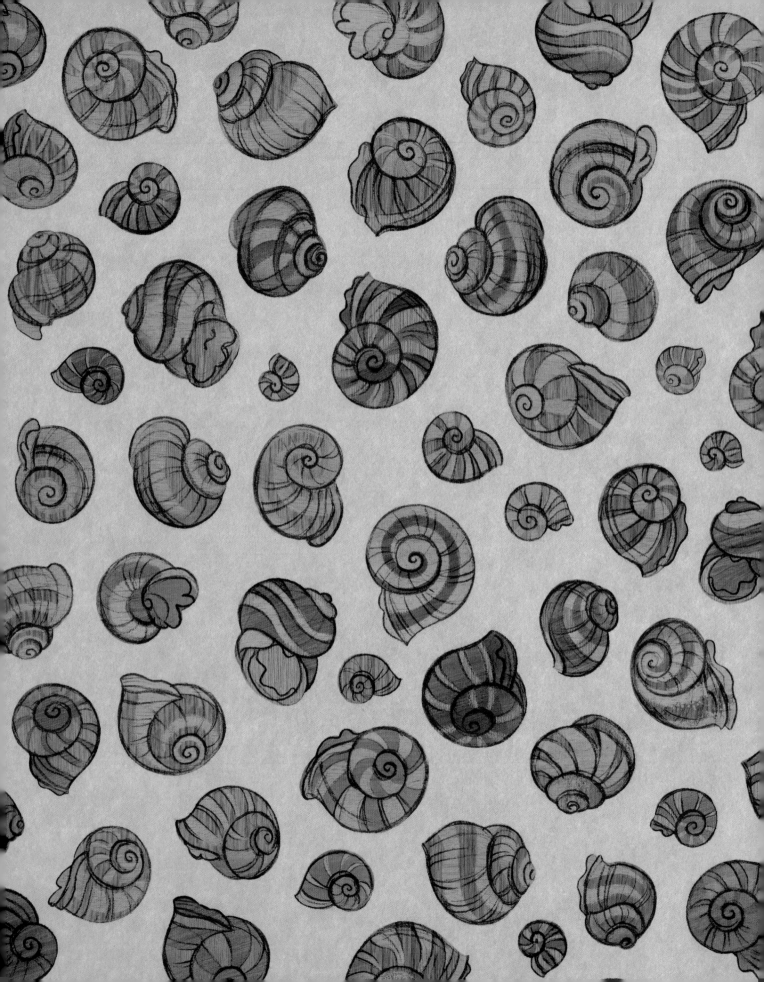